STARTING SPORT

Cricket

Rebecca Hunter

Photography by Chris Fairclough

W

FRANKLIN WATTS

LONDON•SYDNEY

First published in 2006 by
Franklin Watts
338 Euston Road
London NW1 3BH

Franklin Watts Australia
Hachette Children's Books
Level 17/207 Kent Street
Sydney NSW 2000

ISBN-10: 0 7496 6902 0
ISBN-13: 978 0 7496 6902 7

Dewey classification number: 796.358

A CIP catalogue record for this book is available
from the British Library.

Planning and production by Discovery Books Limited
Editor: Rebecca Hunter
Designer: Ian Winton
Photography: Chris Fairclough
Consultant: Jim Foulerton

The author, packager and publisher would like to thank the following
people for their participation in this book: the headmaster, staff and pupils
of Hereford Cathedral Junior School, Hereford.

Printed in China

Franklin Watts is a division of Hachette Children's Books

Contents

The game of cricket

The game of cricket started several hundred years ago in England. Now it is played all over the world from the West Indies to Australia.

Cricket is played on a grass pitch with two teams of 11 players. One team fields and the other team bats. The batting team tries to score as many **runs** as possible. The **fielding** team tries to get the batsmen out as quickly as possible. The team that scores the most runs wins.

Equipment

To play cricket you will need several pieces of equipment:

- The bat is usually made of willow and should be the right size and weight for your age and height.
- The ball is a hard ball with a casing of leather. Younger players often play with a rubber ball.
- The **wicket** is made up of three **stumps** with two **bails** balanced on top.

Bails

Stumps

Kit

Cricketers usually dress in white trousers, shirt and sweater. Batsmen and wicketkeepers wear leg pads, gloves, a **box** and sometimes a helmet. Cricket boots have spikes on the soles for a good grip on grass.

The pitch

Play takes place on a grass field. In the centre is the pitch. The pitch is 20m long and 2.64m wide with a wicket at each end. The pitch is marked out with lines called **creases**. These tell the two batsmen and bowler where to stand or run.

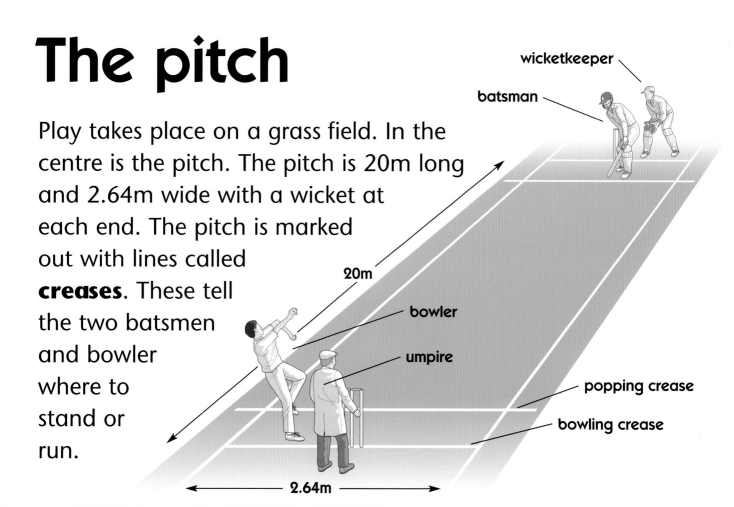

wicketkeeper

batsman

20m

bowler

umpire

popping crease

bowling crease

2.64m

The bowling crease is the line on which the wicket stands and the popping crease is 1.22m in front of this line. The batsman stands far enough in front of the wicket so as not to hit it. The bowler must not put a foot over the popping crease when he lets go of the ball to bowl.

8

The umpire

The umpire is in charge of the game and stands behind the stumps at the bowler's end. In professional cricket games there are two umpires.

Scoring runs

When the ball is hit, the batsman has to run between the wickets to score runs. His bat must touch the ground over the popping crease to score a run.

Surrounding the cricket field is an oval-shaped boundary line. A ball hit over the boundary scores 4 runs if it bounces first and 6 if it is hit straight over.

Fielding

The fielding side of 11 players will have a bowler, wicketkeeper and 9 fielders. The captain decides where on the field the fielders should stand.

Playing a match

A cricket match is an exciting event. Two batsmen come on to the pitch at a time to play an **innings**. An innings is the time they spend playing until they are out. The bowler tries hard to get the batsman out, bowling from each end of the pitch in groups of six bowls, known as **overs**. The batting team's innings is over when ten of the eleven batsmen are out.

Being out

There are many different ways to be out in cricket. These are the most common:

Caught out: a fielder catches the ball after it has been hit and before it bounces.

Run out: a fielder or wicketkeeper (right) breaks the stumps with the ball before the batsman crosses the popping crease with his bat as he tries to score a run.

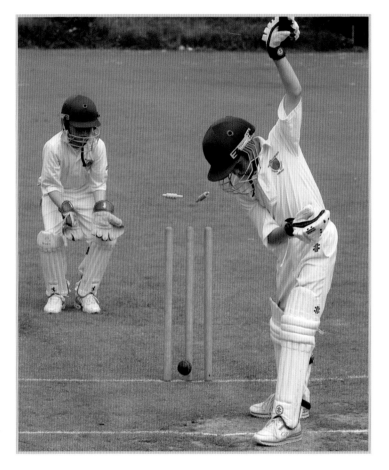

Bowled: the bowler bowls a ball that the batsman misses and which hits the stumps (left).

Leg before wicket (LBW): The ball hits the batsman's pads, when it would otherwise have gone on to hit the wicket.

Hit wicket: the batsman (right) hits the stumps when trying to play a shot.

Batting

Holding the bat

If you are a right-handed batsman hold the bat in this way. Put both hands close together in the middle of the handle. Your right hand should be below your left hand. If you are left handed, your left hand should be below the right.

Stance

How you stand is called your **stance**. Stand with your feet side by side and shoulder-width apart. Your knees should be slightly bent. Keep your head still with your eyes level and looking towards the bowler. Your bat should be just behind the foot nearest the wicket (the 'back foot').

How to swing the bat

Stand still and don't move your head or the rest of your body. When the ball is bowled, move your arms back away from your body and swing the bat back towards the wicket. (Be careful not to hit it!) Step forward and, with your eye on the ball, bring the bat forward to hit it.

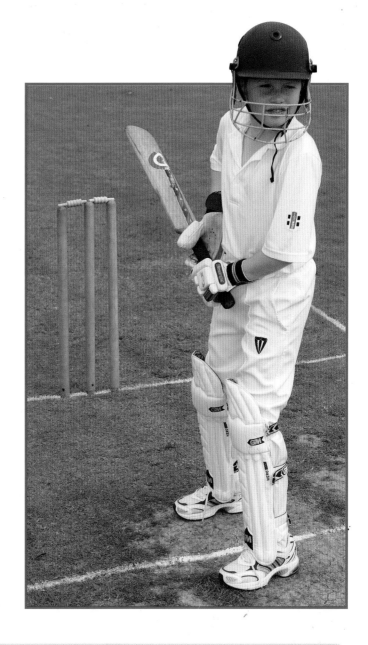

Straight drive

Practise hitting a basic shot or straight drive using a ball and a plastic tee. Place the ball on the tee. Push the bat back and step forward. Now swing through and hit the ball. Follow through with your arms and bat.

Bowling

Overarm bowling

A ball that is going to be bowled can be held like this (right):

The action of an overarm bowl is known as 'drawing the six'. This is because the bowling hand describes a figure '6' as the action is done (see below).

1

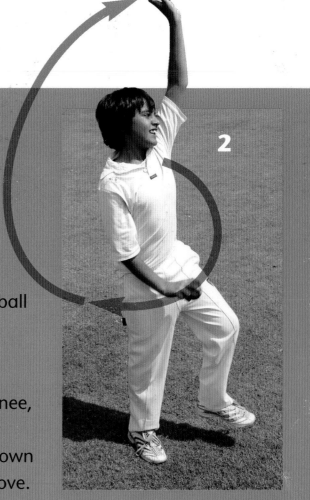

2

1. Raise your non-bowling arm as high as possible. The bowling hand is held in front of your body with the ball near your chin.

2. Raise your knee, and bring your bowling arm down in a circular move.

Hit the stumps

Practise your bowling skills with your friends by setting up a double wicket at one end of the pitch. Take turns at bowling the ball overarm to try and hit the stumps. If the ball hits the wicket you score 4 runs.

3. Stamp the raised foot and swing the bowling arm around behind you.

4. Bring the bowling arm over your head and release the ball. Remember the bowling arm must be straight.

Fielding

A good fielder should be good at throwing, catching and stopping a ball.

Close catching

The correct stance for close catching (catching a ball from a nearby player) is to stand with your feet shoulder-width apart and your hands out in front. The 'heels' of your hands should be close together. Get a friend to throw some underarm balls at you. Catch the ball by wrapping your fingers around it and drawing the ball into your body.

Catching a high ball

To catch a high ball you need to hold your hands in front of you at eye level with your fingers pointing away from your body forming a cup. Keep your eye on the ball and as you catch it, draw the ball into your body.

Catching a flat ball

For this type of catch form your hands into a cup with the thumbs crossed and your fingers pointing up. You must watch the ball carefully and move into the right position to catch it. Draw the ball to the side of your head as you catch.

Practise all these catches with a friend over a distance of 5m increasing to 10m.

17

Wicketkeeping

The wicketkeeper's job is to field any balls that the batsman misses. He is also well positioned to get the batsman out.

If you are the wicketkeeper you must stand behind the wicket. You should be crouched on the balls of your feet. Your hands should be together on the ground with your fingers pointing down. Your head should be upright with your eyes level.

As wicketkeeper you have to judge what sort of ball the bowler will bowl and where you should stand to catch it. Keepers and bowlers need to work together.

Getting the batsman out

The wicketkeeper can get the batsman out in several ways. If the batsman **edges** the ball and the keeper catches it before it hits the ground, the batsman is caught out (below right). If the batsman misses the ball and steps over the popping crease, the wicketkeeper can catch it and break the stumps. The keeper can also stump the batsman as he tries to score runs.

WARNING!
If a hard ball is used, the keeper must wear gloves, pads, a box and helmet.

Batting techniques

Being a good batsman is not just about hitting the ball. It takes many years of practice and good timing to learn how to hit the ball at the right moment.

A good batsman must be able to decide whether to score runs with his hit, or whether to defend the wicket and not be bowled out.

Selecting a shot

When the ball is bowled, as the batsman, you first have to judge the **length** of the ball and decide how to play the shot. If the ball is bowled to a good length (bouncing close to you), you will have to move forward to play your shot.

If it is a short ball (bouncing further away from you), you should stay back to hit it as it will bounce higher.

Defending the wicket

Sometimes the batsman has to play a defensive shot to stop the ball hitting the wicket (right).

For this shot you hold your bat in the path of the ball and allow the ball to hit the bat and drop down. You are not trying to hit the ball, you are just stopping it. This shot does not win you runs but keeps you in the game.

Bowling to win

Warming up

A bowler must warm up well before a game. Jogging around the field will loosen up your leg muscles.

Stretch your arm and shoulder muscles by holding them in these positions.

Running up to bowl

Using the overarm 'six' technique, (see pages 14-15), a run-up should follow these stages:

1. Run and jump off foot, throw arms in air.

Bowling techniques

Bowlers can try and make use of the ball's 'seam' – the stitching around the ball – to make the path of the ball move off a straight line while in the air.

A **spin** bowler will throw the ball higher so that it stays longer in the air and has more chance to spin when it bounces.

A good bowler will keep the batsman guessing what type of ball he is going to bowl.

2. Land in the overarm bowling position and release the ball.

2

3. Make sure the arm follows through and the foot doesn't cross the popping crease.

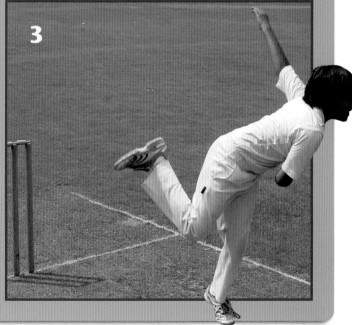

3

Fielding skills

Everyone on a cricket team has to be able to field. A good fielder must be able to stop, catch and throw a ball well.

The 'crow hop'

This throw will help you develop a longer and more powerful overarm throw. Practise it with a friend. The friend rolls a ball to you. Pick it up between your feet. Stand up and cross your right foot behind your left. This will give you a strong throwing position. Step forward with your left foot as you throw.

Stopping a rolling ball

When a ball is rolling very fast along the ground you need to be sure of stopping it. Get behind the ball and kneel down on one knee. Form a cup with your hands. If your hands miss the ball, your body should stop it going on past.

Cricket throwling skills

This game will help develop your throwing and aiming skills. You need two teams of three or four players. Draw two lines about 3m apart. The two teams stand behind the lines and a football is placed in the gap between them. Each player has a tennis ball and should throw their ball at the football to try and knock it over the other team's line. Each time the ball crosses the line, a 'run' is scored.

Junior games

Proper cricket is played with a hard ball which can be difficult for young players to throw and catch. Softball cricket is a much easier way for younger players to learn the game.

Kwik Cricket

Kwik Cricket is a game for children aged five and over. It uses lightweight plastic stumps – with no bails, three sizes of bat and two types of soft ball.

French Cricket

This is a good game to practise all the skills needed in cricket: batting, bowling, throwing and catching. You need at least four players. One player is the batsman and stands in the middle of the playing area with a cricket bat. The other players bowl underarm balls at the batsman.

Players can get the batsman out by hitting his or her legs below the knee or catching a hit. Batsmen must not move their feet until after they have hit the ball. When a player picks up a catch they must bowl from where they stand or throw the ball to another player.

Glossary

Bails the two pieces of wood that are balanced on top of the stumps.

Box an abdominal protector worn by batsmen and wicketkeepers.

Creases the white lines that mark out the cricket pitch.

Edges a batsman edges the ball when he just clips the ball with the edge of his bat.

Fielding the fielding team are the team who are not batting and who are out in the field trying to get the batsmen out.

Innings either one batsman's length of time at the wicket, or the whole batting side's length of time playing.

Length where the ball pitches down the wicket. Lengths can be short, full or good.

Overs groups of six balls bowled. The end of the pitch from which the bowler is bowling changes after each over.

Runs the batsman scores a run when he gets to the end of the pitch without being run out or caught out.

Stance the position the batsman and wicketkeeper stand in whilst waiting for the bowler to bowl.

Stumps the three pieces of wood that, together with the bails, make up the wicket.

Wicket the stumps and bails at each end of the pitch.

Further reading

Know Your Sport: Cricket, Chris Oxlade, Franklin Watts, 2006

Cricket: Essential Sports, Andy Smith, Heinemann Library, 2003

Today's Young Cricketers: A Skills Improvement Manual, Kerry Wedd, Quiller Press, 2001

Book for Young Cricketers, Darren Gough, Hodder & Stoughton Ltd, 1996

Further information

The England and Wales Cricket Board
Lord's Cricket Ground
London
NW8 8QZ
Website: www.ecb.co.uk

Cricket Australia
60 Jolimont Street
Jolimont
Victoria 3002
Australia
Website: www.cricket.com.au

Australian Sports Commission
PO Box 176
Belconnen ACT 2616
Australia
Website: www.ausport.gov.au

Index

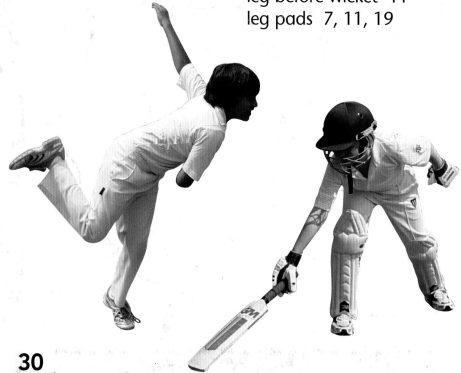